playtime!

hundreds of creative, easy-to-do activities

Text by
Jane B. Mason
Sarah Hines Stephens

Photos by
Aimée Herring

FOG CITY PRESS

Contents

about gymboree

A pioneer in promoting the educational benefits of play, Gymboree has a simple philosophy: fun-filled play is the ideal way to give kids a great start in life. Designed by child-development experts, Gymboree classes and the creative activities featured in the this book help children learn as they play. Offering parent-child interactive programs since 1976, Gymboree Play & Music Centers are now located in more than 30 countries.

a note to parents

The activities in this book are designed for children ages three and older. Please take every precaution to ensure that your child is safe when doing the activities. While we have made every effort to make certain that the information in this book is accurate and reliable, and that the activities are safe and workable with adult supervision, please assess your own child's suitability for a particular activity before attempting it. We disclaim all liability for any unintended, unforeseen, or improper application of the suggestions featured in this book.

Why Play is Good

Playtime is not just fun and games. It's much more!
When you share a silly song, wiggle with abandon, or paint a pirate
hat together, your child is imagining, creating, and making memories—just
to name a few of the benefits. Through play, children learn and hone essential
physical, cognitive, and social skills. They strengthen their bodies, discover their talents,
and explore their emotions as they enjoy the wonders of the world around them.

Playing together is one of the best ways to let your child know how much she means to
you. Bonds are deepened and creative possibilities abound when you hunt for hidden treasure,
blow clouds of bubbles, or pound out a beat together. Play dates will come and go as your
little one grows, but you will always be the favored and most important play partner.

Filled with inspiring activities, this book is designed to make playtime an extraordinary
celebration for you and your youngster. These pages are full of recipes for cooking
up the most delightful playtimes imaginable. Each activity is designed to inspire
confidence and foster imagination, and when you encourage your child to add
his or her own ideas to the mix, you will be supporting creativity and
promoting self-esteem, too. So get ready, get set…let's play!

Gena

Gena Segno
Program Director
Gymboree Play & Music

get moving

Stretch your child's growing body and you will also stretch her mind. In addition to physical benefits, creative movement encourages imagination and provides an outlet for expressing emotions. When your little one moves about, she releases excess energy and builds her sense of balance, body awareness, and gross motor control. Whether done independently, in a group, or with her favorite dance partner (you!) creative movement is a wonderful form of self-expression.

stretch out

Stretching warms up your muscles and gets your body ready for activity. Together with your child, stand with your legs out wide. Reach up high with your hands and then slowly lower your arms to shoulder height and reach or rock from side to side.

Raise your hands up again and pretend to pluck clouds out of the air. Next reach down to pick some imaginary flowers. Wave your arms back and forth over your heads to make rainbows, and then go ahead and reach for the sky.

sit and stretch

Seated on the ground with your child, bend your legs and bring your feet together for a sitting stretch. Gently flap your legs like wings. For an even bigger stretch, slowly lean forward and try to touch your feet with your foreheads.

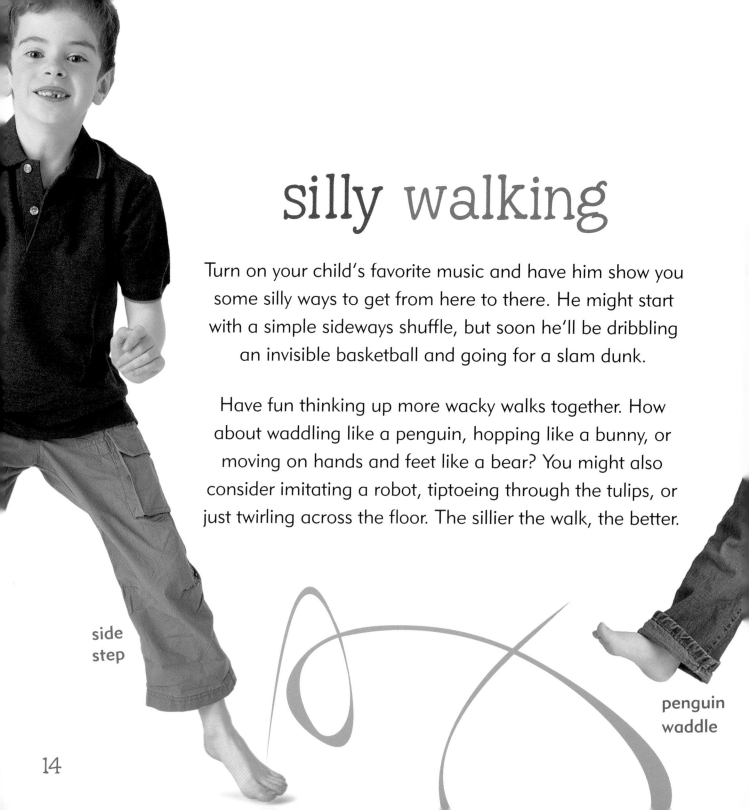

silly walking

Turn on your child's favorite music and have him show you some silly ways to get from here to there. He might start with a simple sideways shuffle, but soon he'll be dribbling an invisible basketball and going for a slam dunk.

Have fun thinking up more wacky walks together. How about waddling like a penguin, hopping like a bunny, or moving on hands and feet like a bear? You might also consider imitating a robot, tiptoeing through the tulips, or just twirling across the floor. The sillier the walk, the better.

side
step

penguin
waddle

bunny
hop

ball
dribble

15

get ready, get set, get down

Celebrate your child's love of movement by dancing with her whenever you can. Just adding music can turn an everyday moment into a dance party. Boogie together in the kitchen while you wash the dishes. Hum and sway while waiting in a long line, or stretch your legs with some silly walking after a car ride. On rainy days, get off the couch and get down. Besides being great ways to channel your child's energy, movement and dance help promote skills such as balance, body awareness, self-confidence, and self-expression.

Your child doesn't care if you're the best dancer in the world or if you have two left feet. She just wants to dance with you! So find your own rhythm, let your child be your guide, and dance the day away.

bubble-chase

The chance to chase wobbly, shimmering bubbles—along with each rewarding *pop!*—offers kids a great motivation to get moving.

Popping bubbles is a sure-to-please activity when children of different ages are playing together. Babies as young as three months can build sensory awareness, eye-hand coordination, and an understanding of cause and effect as their eyes follow, and their hands reach for, floating bubbles.

Talking to the older kids about their bubble-blowing discoveries, such as what it feels like to pop a bubble, supports language development.

b is for bubble

To the tune of
"C is for Cookie"

B is for bubble, bubble, bubble.
B is for bubble, that's good enough for me.
B is for bubble, bubble, bubble.
Oh, bubble, bubble, bubble starts with B!

P is for pop 'em, pop 'em, pop 'em.
P is for pop 'em, that's good enough for me.
P is for pop 'em, pop 'em, pop 'em.
Oh, pop 'em, pop 'em, pop 'em starts with P!

round and round

Ring dances work well for just two dancers or a whole crowd. Have your child or a group of children hold hands or share scarves and walk around in a circle with you. Start the game off with "Ring Around the Rosy," and after you "all fall down," sing the second verse below to get everyone in the circle to stand back up.

With older kids, you can sing new songs, change direction, and alter the pace. Or come into the center, raise your arms, and give a cheer when you meet in the middle, then swoosh back out into a circle.

ring around the rosy

Ring around the rosy

Pocketful of posies.

Ashes, ashes,

We all fall down!

The cows are in the meadow
Eating buttercups.

Sleeping, sleeping…

They all stand up!

dancers in a ring

To the tune of "The Wheels on the Bus"

The dancers in the ring go round and round,
Round and round, round and round.
The dancers in the ring go round and round,
All fall down!
The dancers in the ring go up and down,
Up and down, up and down.
The dancers in the ring go up and down,
All fall down!
The dancers in the ring go in and out,
In and out, in and out.
The dancers in the ring go in and out,
All fall down!

stomp!

Is your child in the mood to make some musical noise? Get a beat going with some shoes made for stomping! Ditch the sneakers in favor of a pair of good old rain boots or dressy shoes with hard heels. See how stomps sound on different surfaces such as wood, carpet, or tile. Try bubble wrap!

For variety, older children can add the swish of a broom to the mix. Younger kids can clap or pat their bodies. Create a simple rhythm with clapping hands, clomping feet, or sweeping broom strokes and ask your child to echo it back. Then reverse roles and copy her rhythm.

make it!

Help your little tapper create her own tap shoes by gluing canning-jar lids onto the soles of a pair of shoes. Have her tap on tile or concrete—just avoid floors that get scratched easily.

pop me!

Chasing and popping bubbles always makes for active fun.
For variety, try adding a little more creative body movement.

Blow a big batch of bubbles and invite your child to try to
pop as many as she can. Encourage her to pop them using
different parts of her body. The top of the head, fingers,
and feet are favorite bubble-poppers, but elbows, knees,
shoulders, and noses do the job nicely, too. This activity
boosts her body awareness and encourages her to enjoy the
feeling of making things happen by using her body.

After she's tried several options, ask her which body
parts she likes using the best and why. Talking about her
discoveries helps develop her language skills.

popping bubbles

To the tune of "Allouette"

Popping bubbles, I like popping bubbles,
Popping bubbles, it's so fun for me.

Can you pop them on your knee?
Can you pop them on your knee?
On your knee, on your knee,
Oooooh…

Popping bubbles, I like popping bubbles,
Popping bubbles, fun for you and me.

limbo

How low can you go? Limbo is a great way for a group of kids to find out. Ask two kids to stretch several knotted-together scarves between them at shoulder height. Crank up the music and have the dancers take turns bending backward to go underneath. Lower the scarves slightly each time everyone has had a turn.

Bend the rules and let the kids get creative. Younger children can crawl or roll under, while older ones can crab walk.

limbo, limbo

to the tune of "Twinkle, Twinkle, Little Star"

Limbo, limbo, way down low,

Bend your body as you go.

Try to make it all the way,

Without touching while you play.

Limbo, limbo, way down low,

Bend your body as you go.

hula hips

Hawaiian dancers tell stories with their movements.
You can help your child tell an island story, too. Begin
making waves together by moving your hands and arms
up and down. Sway your bodies like palm trees in the wind
and practice moving your hips in a circle. Ask your child
to show you how he would dance to tell the story of a
shark. How about a waterfall or a volcano?

Play off the Hawaiian theme by wearing a grass skirt. You
can add colorful flowers to a premade one or make your
own by tying strips of fabric, raffia, or ribbons onto a belt.

funky chicken

shake a tail feather

Farm animals have some great moves, and you and your child can do them, too. By turning your arms into flapping wings (just tuck your thumbs in your armpits), you can do the funky chicken together. Or how about the horse trot? Just pick up your feet and move to a galloping rhythm. Don't forget to hold onto the reins!

horse trot

animal farm

Try a new take on "Old MacDonald" using animal movements instead of noises: chicken/peck, horse/trot, dog/wag, duck/waddle.

Old MacDonald had a farm, E-I-E-I-O.

And on his farm he had a frog, E-I-E-I-O.
With a hop, hop, here and a hop, hop, there.
Here a hop, there a hop.
Everywhere a hop, hop!
Old MacDonald had a farm, E-I-E-I-O.

dragon dance

Do an easy version of a traditional Chinese dragon dance by covering three or more children with a long piece of lightweight fabric or a bedsheet and tying a knot near the end to make a tail. Play music or have another child beat a drum while the dancers move together under the fabric, alternating between standing tall and crouching low. You can even ask the dragon "head" (the first person) to try to catch the "tail" (the last person) without breaking the dragon formation.

chinese dragon

To the tune of "Frère Jacques"

Chinese dragon, Chinese dragon,
Stretch and bend, stretch and bend.
Try to catch the tail, try to catch the tail.
We're all friends, we're all friends.

make music

Tips

Repetition is key to learning, so repeat songs and other activities at least twice.

•

To unify you and your child, clap out a steady beat when you're singing together.

•

Ease transitions and create family rituals using music—lullabies for bedtime, then counting songs for getting ready in the morning.

Team up with your little musician to fill every day with songs and sounds. Whether you're making music together or just listening, you'll help him build memory, language, and pre-math skills. From drumming to strumming, singing to swaying, music play also fosters self-expression and creativity. Exposure to different musical styles gives your child an opportunity to define his own tastes. These musically-inspired activities will be just right for the future Mozart or full-on rock star.

37

listen, sing & shout

Share the joy of music with your child by frequently listening to different styles—such as classical, country, or rock—together. Listen for elements that make each style distinct: special rhythms, instruments, or musical patterns. For example, marching music provides a strong underlying beat. Folk music tells a story. Jazz embraces improvisation, creating one-of-a-kind performances.

Play your young fan's newfound favorites and make listening an interactive game by clapping, walking, or dancing to the beat.

music activity

Try a game of "what's my line" with your favorite recorded music. Pause a familiar song in the middle and invite your child to shout out the next few words—or better yet, make up some new lyrics together.

sing-alongs!

Down by the Banks of the Hanky Panky

Down by the banks
of the hanky panky,
where the bullfrogs jump
from bank to banky.
They went oops, opps, belly flops.
One missed the lily pad
and went . . . kerplop!

Head, Shoulders, Knees, and Toes

Head, shoulders,
knees, and toes.
Knees and toes!

Head, shoulders,
knees, and toes.
Knees and toes!

Eyes and ears and
mouth and nose.
Head, shoulders,
knees, and toes.
Knees and toes!

Pop Goes the Weasel

All around the cobbler's bench,
the monkey chased the weasel,
the monkey thought
it was all in fun,
POP goes the weasel!

shake it up

The sound of a shaking maraca is enough to get any child moving—whether it's one you have on hand, or one she has made herself (with a little help from an adult, of course).

Together with your child, shake the maracas in the air or tap them gently against different parts of your bodies. Experiment with a variety of shakes: superfast for a constant rattle, or nice and slow for a single, repetitive sound. Put on her favorite recorded music and shake to the beat. Play a game of stop-and-go shaking or make up your own crazy rhythm!

make it!

Raid the pantry to create maracas with your child. Partially fill empty water bottles or plastic storage containers with pasta, dried beans, or rice. Seal the tops securely. Then get shaking!

water music

Make music right in your own kitchen! Simply set out several glasses filled with varying amounts of water. Give your child a chopstick or wooden spoon and ask him to gently tap the glasses. Listen to the notes he plays and talk about them. Which one is highest? How are the sounds alike? How are they different?

Together, arrange the glasses in order, from low to high. (The more water in the glass, the lower the note.) Then make a "water xylophone" using several same-size drinking glasses and graduated amounts of water. To play a rough musical scale, experiment with the water levels until you get six or eight notes, each one higher than the one before. Tap out a familiar tune like "Twinkle, Twinkle, Little Star," or invite your aspiring musician to compose his own song by rearranging the glasses and exploring different rhythms.

marching band

make it!

Oatmeal containers and paper-towel rolls make great bandleader hats and batons. Have your child decorate them with colored paper, adding fringe and musical details.

Get ready to march! Turn on some parade-inspiring music and have your child grab whatever instrument is on hand—or improvise with a few items from the kitchen cupboard. She can blow into a paper towel roll, clang pot lids together like cymbals, or pound on the lid or bottom of a plastic storage container.

Take turns being the bandleader with a baton made from a decorated paper-towel roll, a wrapping-paper roll, or a poster tube. March together around your house, your yard, or all the way to the park.

workin' on the railroad

I've been workin' on the railroad
All the livelong day.
I've been workin' on the railroad
Just to pass the time away.
Don't you hear the whistle blowing?
Rise up so early in the morn.
Don't you hear the captain shouting,
"Dinah, blow your horn."

Dinah, won't you blow,
Dinah, won't you blow,
Dinah, won't you blow your horn?

Someone's in the kitchen with Dinah.
Someone's in the kitchen I know.
Someone's in the kitchen with Dinah,
Strummin' on the old banjo.
Singin' "Fee fi fiddly-i-o,
Fee fi fiddly-i-o, fee fi fiddly-i-o,"
Strummin' on the old banjo.

strum fun

You and your child can make a guitar from a small cardboard box (or even just a sturdy lid). First cut a hole in the center of the box or lid to create the body of the guitar. Make a narrow slit on the top edge and slide a second strong piece of cardboard through to act as the neck. Use tape or glue to secure the neck and then cut a few notches at the end to hold the rubber-band strings in place.

Wrap extra-large rubber bands across the opening and up over the neck, making sure they are snug but not too tight. (A quick alternative is to wrap a few rubber bands around a plastic bowl.) Then get ready to do some serious strumming!

jug band jam

Help your child form an old-fashioned jug band! With a small crowd, a little help, and a few basic materials, kids can create a slew of instruments. (To create a rubber band–strung banjo, see "Strum Fun" on page 49 and follow the guitar instructions.)

Make a tambourine by having your young music maker put jingle bells or dried beans between two paper plates. Staple or stitch the plates together securely. Alternatively, older musicians can stitch a whole ring of bells around the edge of a single paper plate.

For a jug, provide a clean plastic bottle without a lid. Blow across the hole at the top to make a deep whistling sound.

To create a kazoo, cover the end of a cardboard tube with wax paper, secure it with a rubber band, and hum or sing into the tube.

To build a washboard, find a piece of heavy corrugated cardboard and help your child carefully remove the outer paper layer on one side, exposing the ridges. Rub up and down the ridges with a smooth stick or the handle of a wooden spoon to make music.

strum and blow

To the tune of "The Mulberry Bush"

This is the way we strum and blow,
Strum and blow, strum and blow,
This is the way we strum and blow,
So early in the morning.

This is the way we clang and bang,
Clang and bang, clang and bang,
This is the way we clang and bang,
So early in the morning.

world beat

Nearly every culture has a tradition of pounding out a rhythm, from the tall talking drums of Africa to the giant taiko drums native to Japan. Your child can move to the beat of her own drum, too.

Try making drums of different sizes with your little percussionist and explore the varied sounds they make. Use empty oatmeal containers, wooden or metal bowls, or plastic tubs. And don't forget the drumsticks! Chopsticks, spoons, hands, or even a wire whisk all make distinct percussive sounds.

music activity

Your child can use the drums to tap out the syllables in the names of favorite people, pets, or family members, such as Grand-ma or Aun-tie Bea. You can also tap out ways to say hello in different languages, such as *ho-la* (oh-la, Spanish) or *jam-bo* (jaum-bo, Swahili).

count it!

Once your child is one year or older, introduce him to counting with plenty of bubbles and a fun bubbly song.

Show him how to pop bubbles by poking them with his finger or clapping them between his hands. Sing and count out his popping successes together.

The repetition in this song is great for language development, and the bubbles turn counting into a gleeful game.

pop-pop-pop

To the tune of
"Ten Little Indians"

1 little, 2 little, 3 little bubbles,
4 little, 5 little, 6 little bubbles,
7 little, 8 little, 9 little bubbles,
10 little bubbles go pop!

Pop-pop-pop those bubbles,
Pop-pop-pop those bubbles,
Pop-pop-pop those bubbles,
Pop some bubbles with me!

cut a demo

i love singing

To the tune of "Frère Jacques"

I love singing,
I love singing.

Yes I do!
Yes I do!

I made up this song,
You can sing along.

Me and you!
Me and you!

Your child will shine in the spotlight when she records and performs her own song.

Help her choose a familiar favorite and change the words to create a silly song about family, friends, or even a cherished pet. Then use your computer, video camera, or tape recorder to capture her performance. She'll love playing the recording and hearing herself sing—and might even decide to do an encore!

play a game

Tips

Keep directions consistent, so your child can master the game more easily and enjoy the feeling of success.

•

Games should be played in the spirit of exploration and fun, never competition. Explain that each participant is a winner, start to finish.

•

Choose age-appropriate games to avoid frustration.

Extremely versatile, games can entertain a single person or many. They help children develop skills such as counting, shape and color recognition, and spatial relations. When your child participates in a game, she engages in parallel play while learning to follow directions and being part of a team. Open-ended games that include songs and a variety of props give children the opportunity to initiate ideas and anticipate outcomes, building confidence and a love of learning.

61

ground games

If you and your child are aiming to have a good time (and work on eye-hand coordination), a colorful target is just the thing. Draw a circle surrounded by rings and fill them in together. Find small beanbags or plastic bottle caps to throw. Pick a spot to toss from, mark it with chalk, and take turns trying to get a bull's-eye.

personalize tic-tac-toe game pieces with chalk

A classic game such as tic-tac-toe takes on a new twist when you draw an oversize board on the ground. Cut large-scale Xs and Os from cardboard or buy premade letters at a crafts store. For extra fun, paint the game pieces with chalkboard paint and decorate.

table topper

If you don't have a large outdoor space, or bad weather is keeping you inside, your little one can draw a checkerboard, a smaller target, or a tic-tac-toe grid on a regular chalkboard laid flat or on a kids' table coated with chalkboard paint.

63

dodge-a-bubble

Here's a more-the-merrier dodging game. And while the players are running, dodging, and giggling, they'll also be improving their balance, body awareness, and coordination.

Gather the gang in a circle with one child in the middle. Hand out wands that have been primed with bubble solution and ask the kids to blow bubbles into the center of the circle. The child in the middle tries to dodge the floating bubbles for as long as he possibly can.

Once a bubble bursts or lands on him, he joins the circle, and another child takes his place in the center of the bubble-dodging action.

monkey see, monkey move

Playing copycat is a great way to get moving and a fun activity for two children, or for you and your child, to do together. Invite one partner to make a surprised, sad, or silly face—or maybe even a monkey face! Then ask the other player to mimic the expression to create a mirror image.

Build on the game by adding hand and body movements. Kids might want to imitate animals—by swishing their tails, for instance—or simply give themselves a pat on the head.

say, say, oh playmate

Say, say, oh playmate,
Come out and play with me,
And bring your dollies three,
Climb up my apple tree.
Slide down my rain barrel,
Into my cellar door,
And we'll be jolly friends,
Forever more, more, more, more.

So sorry, playmate,
I cannot play with you,
My dolly has the flu,
Boo hoo hoo hoo hoo hoo.
I have no rain barrel,
I have no cellar door,
But we'll be jolly friends,
Forever more, more, more, more.

clap together

Remember "Say, Say, Oh Playmate" (left) or "Down by the Banks of the Hanky Panky" (see page 41)? These clapping games are as much fun today as they were decades ago.

Teach your child one of the simple rhyming songs, and then add clapping rhythms and crossovers for plenty of fun and silliness. You can modify the clapping patterns to make them easier to follow. Younger children can simply hold up their hands for you to clap, or tap their knees along to the song.

bubble and spoon

Here's a chance to run an "egg"-and-spoon race that's not so messy—and it helps build coordination and self-confidence, too.

For the host: Gather all the players, designate a start and a finish line (for instance, from the house to the back of the yard), hand out plastic spoons, and fill the air with bubbles.

For the "bubble and spooners": Catch a falling bubble on your plastic spoon and, with careful steps, aim for the finish line. Bubble still unpopped when you reach it? Then you're a winner!

materials

- bubble solution
- bubble wand
- plastic spoons (bubbles don't last as long on metal)

catch a bubble

To the tune of "Allouette"

Catch a bubble, can you catch a bubble?
Catch a bubble on your little spoon.

Catch a bubble way up high,
Catch a bubble way down low.
Way up high, way down low…
Oooooooh…

Catch a bubble, can you catch a bubble?
Catch a bubble on your little spoon.

dot-to-dot

Dot-to-dot is a great game for a couple of kids or a whole crew; plus it builds spatial awareness and coordination. To create the play space, have each child choose a chalk color and draw dots—large enough to stand upon—on a patio or sidewalk.

When the playing field is finished, invite each child to have a turn calling out directions to the others. The caller can use a spinner or make up creative ways for the players to move—"dance to a red circle," "hop to a yellow circle," or "run around a blue circle"—changing the colors and movements each time.

make it!

Create a spinner using a square of dark cardboard. Draw dots in a circle—one dot for each color of chalk on the playing field. Then make an indicator by affixing a craft stick in the center with a fastener that can turn. Or simply put colored circles in a hat and have each caller pull one out.

floating bubbles

To the tune of "Frère Jacques"

Floating bubbles, floating bubbles,
Way up high, in the sky.
See the pretty bubbles,
Pretty little bubbles,
Way up high, in the sky.

all the pretty bubbles

*To the tune of
"Did You Ever See a Lassie"*

All the pretty bubbles, the bubbles, the bubbles,
All the pretty bubbles go way up high.

There are big ones and tiny ones and
small ones and shiny ones.

See the pretty bubbles go way up high!

bubble clouds

What's more fun than just one little bubble?
An irresistabubble cloud of shimmering bubbles!

So invite kids three years old and up to blow as many
bubbles as they can for 10 seconds. Once bubbles
fill the air have the kids use drinking straws to blow the
bubbles higher and farther—and see if they can keep all
the bubbly spheres aloft and heading up into the sky.

Encourage the little ones to work together to keep
their bubble cloud floating high. Get ready for
giggles, glee, and happy chaos as they expand
their social skills and learn to cooperate.

dance…

freeze!

freeze dance

Invite your child to explore the space around her by jumping, skipping, and twirling to music. Ask her to "freeze" in place when you pause the song. You'll both get a good giggle out of the crazy positions she ends up in. Freeze dancing is also an easy and entertaining activity for a whole group of dancers—plus, it helps develop coordination and promotes listening skills.

melt

melt down

Keep the game going by inviting your frozen dancer to "melt" into a puddle on the floor, then restart the music to get her back on her feet.

lily pad hop

Create an easy game by helping your child draw several lily pads on pavement, a patio, or a driveway with water-based paint or chalk. Don't forget the lotus flowers! Once you have a "pondful," get ready to jump.

Little ones will enjoy leaping from one pad to another in a random pattern, while older kids can hop in sequence. Have a leader choose the path and watch the other froggies follow. They'll have a great time jumping, and they'll be building gross-motor skills, spatial awareness, and coordination at the same time.

poppin' those bubbles

To the tune of "Shortenin' Bread"

Poppin' those bubbles, bubbles, bubbles,
Poppin' those bubbles, you and me.

Poppin' them high, poppin' them low,
Poppin' those bubbles, wherever they go.

Poppin' those bubbles, bubbles, bubbles,
Poppin' those bubbles, you and me!

high jump

A bubble high jump is a real crowd-pleaser and a great way to explore spatial awareness with children.

Ask one child to hold a hula hoop out to one side, about chest high, and challenge everyone else to blow bubbles so high that they "jump" through the hoop. If more than one child gets a bubble through the hoop in the first round, make things more challenging by raising it a little higher for the next round.

With lots of budding bubblologists and so many bubbles, this activity is less messy done outdoors. And it will work best if there's little or no wind to blow those bubbles off course.

let's pretend

The power of imagination often fuels the richest playtime, and bringing a make-believe story "to life" engages every aspect of your child's mind and body. Besides the sheer joy of acting out their inner dreams and ideas, children engaged in pretend play learn language and early literacy skills, logical thinking, and social confidence. They also enhance physical skills such as body awareness, strength, and coordination.

ferocious lion or pussycat?

mask menagerie

Are animal games a favorite at your house? Add drama to playtime with easy-to-make masks—and build kids' imagination and thinking skills, too. Help your child cut out animal-face shapes from cardboard or heavy paper to decorate with chalk. A wild mane and whiskers are unmistakably lion, while a wide face with big ears suggests a monkey. Or encourage your child to conjure up fanciful beasts—with unexpected horns, patterns, or features.

When the coloring is complete, glue or tape a craft stick to the bottom of each mask for a handle. Cut out eye holes if your wild thing will be prowling about. Otherwise, kids can peek around the masks or use them as puppets for an impromptu show.

go wild

Transforming your child into a wild animal will give her a chance to reveal her fierce side. Look at animal-themed books for inspiration, then sketch a design together. A wash of orange, a few painted spots, and a muzzle with menacing fangs can turn her into a snarling leopard. Or keep it simple with bold tiger or zebra stripes. You can also add paper or felt ears to a headband and tuck a scarf into her waistband to mimic a swishy tail. And don't forget to take time to grunt, growl, hop, and prowl with your wild one.

step-by-step

To make an easy animal face, start by painting a light-colored muzzle above your child's upper lip and extend it out toward her cheeks. Using a dark color, outline the muzzle, shade the tip of her nose, and add upswept lines to suggest feline eyes. Finish with fangs, darkened lips, and spots to create a whisker effect.

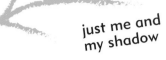

just me and
my shadow

self-portraits

Play dress-up with a twist by helping your creative genius become his own alter ego. Start by talking about what he'd like to be. A robot? A soccer player? A violinist? (This is a great way to build self-awareness, self-esteem, and imagination.) Then outline his body on the pavement by tracing his shadow (if the sun cooperates) or drawing around him while he lies down. Once you've completed the outline, your model can get to work coloring his clothing to match his fantasy.

For more fun with shadows, trace them from several angles. Encourage silliness—hold up a ball to create a two-headed beast, for instance. Or let the sun be your fun-house mirror and trace extra tall or short shadows at different times of day.

spy time

Ask your little secret agent what kind of gadgets she needs to solve her latest case. Special spy glasses? A walkie-talkie wristwatch? Or maybe a sonic radar ring? Then grab trench coats and notepads and go undercover together for some super-sleuthing. Get sneaky with a game of secret-agent hide-and-seek or "I Spy." You might even plant a few clues and help your private investigator go on a treasure hunt.

car wash

Roll up every tricycle, ride-on car, and wagon for a bubbly "car" wash! Muster a work crew of kids and hand out buckets and large soft sponges to each child.

Use a wet sponge to froth a mixture of bubble solution and a splash of water in each bucket so that they all brim with bubbles. Have the kids dip sponges into their bubble-buckets and "wash" away all that backyard dirt. (Always supervise children when they're around water.)

Help the kids blow streams of bubbles into the air, making the yard look just like a real-life car wash. Extend the fun by finding other washable toys to bubble-wash. Perhaps dolly would like it?

materials

- tricycles, ride-on cars, or wagons
- buckets
- large soft sponges
- bubble solution
- bubble wands

this is the way we wash the car

To the tune of
"Here We Go 'Round the Mulberry Bush"

This is the way we wash the car,
Wash the car, wash the car.

This is the way we wash the car,
Come wash the car with me!

woodland creatures

It's not hard to turn a backyard or room into an enchanted world, or a child into a magical creature. With a few painted embellishments, your little one can quickly become a fairy princess, a sprite, or an elf. Or you can simply paint a woodland friend on an arm or a cheek.

Gather a group of your child's friends together and create a fairy kingdom. Ask them to find tiny fairy "houses" hidden among the garden plants. Or help them cover a table with a blanket and have a picnic underneath.

flutterby

Let butterflies inspire a dance session. Give your child a scarf for each hand and invite her to move and imagine the scarves are butterfly wings. (Optionally, set the scene with ballet music.)

Using a larger piece of fabric or a towel, you can also help your little caterpillar roll herself into a cocoon on the floor. Suggest that she lie still for a moment before wriggling free and emerging as a beautiful butterfly. With the fabric serving as her wings, she can choreograph her own fluttery dance.

royal rulers

Is your child feeling regal? Paint elegant, curved lines to create a tiara or crown (see photo on page 2). Or turn her into a dashing knight with a metal helmet fashioned out of a bold outline and plenty of silver paint. For a quick royal treatment, pair a toy crown with rosy cheeks and lips. Invite the castle dwellers to dress up and hold court. Who will they play—rulers, guards, or jesters?

step-by-step

It's easy to bejewel your queen or princess with a painted tiara made from a few simple shapes. In a base color of her choice, paint a heart centered low on her forehead with a teardrop below it. Using the same color, add a curved line and some delicate dots over each eyebrow. Then with a darker color, draw partial outlines beneath these shapes. Finish with white highlights and, if you'd like, other details such as a matching heart necklace.

create a town

With a few boxes, some chalk, and your help, your budding city planner can make his own small-scale chalk town. Start by talking about the buildings—houses, a school, a grocery store, a library, an office tower—that he might want to include, and together map out where they should go on the ground or a large piece of cardboard.

Encourage him to think about and add details, such as roads and train tracks and perhaps a farm or lake at the edge of town. He can also decorate cardboard boxes (paint them ahead of time with black chalkboard paint for extra fun) and use them for buildings, bridges, or tunnels. Have him choose toys, such as cars and boats, to complete the picture, and your urban designer will bring his town to life.

coming in
for a landing

under the sea

Is your child feeling nautical? Invite your seafarer to become a swashbuckling pirate with a painted-on eye patch and mustache. Paint on a bandana or use a fabric one—maybe add a hat. For an underwater adventure, transform your child into a beautiful mermaid with a simple sea-inspired pattern around the eyes (see photo on page 82 for more ideas).

Encourage your seagoer to take a make-believe journey in a washtub or a cardboard-box ship and narrate it along the way. The ocean blue is yours to explore!

step-by-step

To adorn your little one with aquatic embellishments, start with the shape of a sea creature, such as a sea horse. With a light color, paint dots to illustrate air bubbles or the chain of a shell necklace. Finish with contrasting details and colorful outlines.

create art

Tips

Keep art supplies on hand and encourage full exploration—messiness is part of the process!

•

Remember that art doesn't need to resemble something to have value or meaning.

•

Ask your child to tell you about her artwork, then discuss the various colors, shapes, and textures.

Doing arts and crafts together is a multisensory way to share and communicate with your child. Children engaged in the simplest act of applying color to paper or putting hands to clay are learning to plan, predict, design and act—essential skills for critical thinking. Talk about the materials you use and describe how they look, feel, sound, and smell. This will help you respond to your little artist's "masterpieces" and support her creativity in the process.

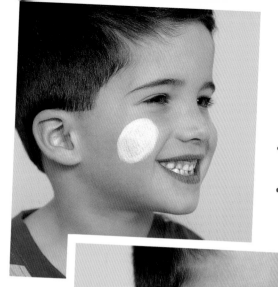

painting basics

Here's an easy approach for creating a quick face-paint design:

1. If you are using face-paint crayons, warm and soften them by doing a practice design on your arm or hand.

2. Draw and fill in a simple shape, like a circle, using a light-toned base color.

3. Embellish your design with details, working from light to dark. You can create new colors by going over the same spot with two different hues.

4. Outline your design with a dark color to help it stand out. Go over your lines several times to achieve a darker edge.

Tip: Painting in front of a mirror will let your child see what you are doing and allow him to do some painting, too.

Tip: Talk about designs with your child and consider sketching them on paper first. You can even cut out a design to make a stencil.

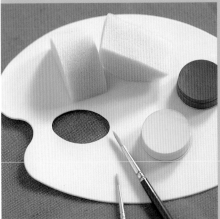

paint palette tips

Here are some tips for using pots of solid paint:

• Work up paints with a brush by swirling in small amounts of water until the paint is the consistency of white craft glue.

• Use makeup sponges to smooth or blot paint onto skin. For a child-friendly size, cut them in half.

• Use wide brushes for large areas and narrower ones for smaller details.

• To make a new color, mix two or more hues in a bowl, on a palette, or on the back of your hand.

 # butterflies

Watch your child's imagination take flight when a butterfly (painted in profile or head-on, showing all four wings) lands on her cheek. If she wants more company, you can add another garden friend, such as a ladybug (see page 109), to her other cheek. Before washing up, your little nature lover can capture a lasting impression of each creature by pressing a piece of paper against it and rubbing gently before carefully peeling the paper away.

step-by-step

For a simple butterfly, start by painting a basic four-winged outline using a light color. Next, use a contrasting color to fill in the wings. Complete the design with a dark outline and antennae. Invite your child to paint more butterflies on her arms, hands, or legs.

 # shape up

For a quick design, ask your child to choose a geometric shape and talk about what that shape could become. Is a circle the outside of a smiley face, or the first step in the outline of a cat's head? (Just add a pair of triangle ears.) A heart "tattooed" on an arm—with the name of someone special—will send a clear message about who is dear to your little one's heart.

Look at books, magazines, or greeting cards—or just around the house—for other design ideas. Keep in mind that arms and legs make easy-to-see canvases for kids to try these shapes on themselves.

step-by-step

Team up with your child to create an out-of-this-world design. Set yourselves up in front of a mirror so that you can admire your handiwork, then help her get started by outlining a star for her to fill in with the same color. Together, add details, such as a colorful tail, and finish with an outline in a darker color. Remember to wish upon your star.

materials needed:
1 cup plaster of paris
½ cup water
powdered tempera paint

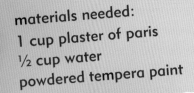

make your own chalk

Making chalk is simple. Begin by gathering materials (see list, above) and helping your child choose molds, such as silicone ice-cube trays, small paper cups, or cardboard tubes. Next mix together plaster and water. To add color, pour in powdered tempera paint and stir to mix. (Note: paint may stain clothes or other surfaces.) Allow the mixture to stand for a few minutes, then spoon it into the molds.

Let the chalk dry completely in the molds. This can take from several hours to a few days, depending on the size of the mold. If the chalk still feels moist when it is removed, allow it to air-dry for an additional day.

chalk rubbings

This classic art project comes to life with colored chalk, paper, and a variety of objects. Help your child gather various items with interesting textures: leaves, bark, melons, keys, sandpaper, bumpy fabric, building toys, crinkled foil. Show your budding artist how to place the paper on top of an item's surface and rub over it gently with the side of the chalk. (Taping items down adds stability.) Compare the results. Identifying similarities and differences helps your child become a critical thinker.

a lasting impression

Rubbing giant letters can be both a tactile and a literary experience. Together with your child, make the sounds of each letter as she transfers it to paper. Ask her to think of words that start with the same sound. You can help her spell out these words, other favorite words, or her name.

117

think big

Concrete patios, driveways, garage doors, and wooden decks are all ready-and-waiting oversize chalk canvases. Discuss theme ideas with your child, then pick one to draw together. Explore the ocean deep in an underwater scene, construct a cityscape, or sculpt a mountain range. This activity stretches a child's imagination and helps hone visual and spatial skills.

To cover a lot of ground, show your child how to use chalk paint and rollers (sold at crafts stores) to fill in a background. With a younger child, you might want to map out a few basic elements to help get things started. When you're done, talk about what you've drawn. Then wash it off and create a new design together; colors are extra vibrant on a damp surface.

paint-a-bubble

Fill a tray halfway with water and add a squirt of dishwashing liquid. Mix in a spoonful of tempera paint and froth by blowing into the mixture with a drinking straw. (Be careful not to suck up any solution!)

Blow until bubbles reach the lip of the tray, then help your child carefully lower a piece of paper onto the bubbly surface and lift it off quickly. Lay the paint-a-bubble masterpiece out on a flat surface for about 30 minutes, or until dry to touch.

materials

- plastic tray, 4 inches (10 cm) deep
- dishwashing liquid
- nontoxic liquid tempera paint
- drinking straw
- heavy white paper

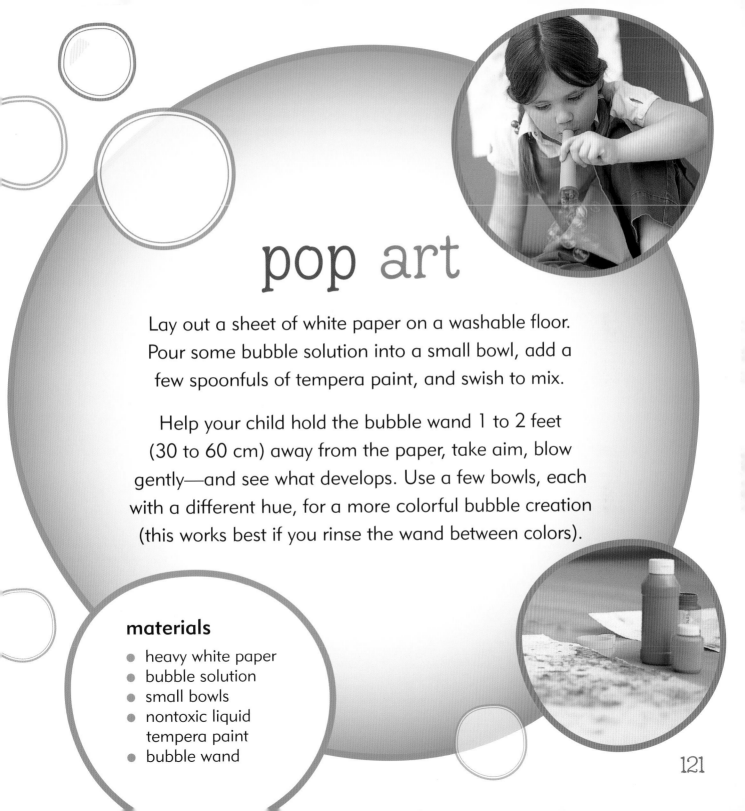

pop art

Lay out a sheet of white paper on a washable floor. Pour some bubble solution into a small bowl, add a few spoonfuls of tempera paint, and swish to mix.

Help your child hold the bubble wand 1 to 2 feet (30 to 60 cm) away from the paper, take aim, blow gently—and see what develops. Use a few bowls, each with a different hue, for a more colorful bubble creation (this works best if you rinse the wand between colors).

materials

- heavy white paper
- bubble solution
- small bowls
- nontoxic liquid tempera paint
- bubble wand

chalk talk

Special greetings—such as a "welcome home" for a parent—have extra impact when the "paper" is a front walkway or porch. Ask your child what she wants to say, then help her get her message across using words, numbers, pictures, or a combination.

She might write a special birthday, holiday, or party greeting on stair risers to be read as the lucky recipient walks up. Or she might illustrate a friendly message on the sidewalk for passersby. Snap a photo of your child with her note so faraway loved ones can share in the fun, too. Opportunities to practice sounding out words and writing letters help your child develop skills needed for reading.

footloose

Let your kids try on painted shoes in whatever style or color they like—anything from ballet slippers to sporty high-tops to beachy flip-flops. How about some red-hot cowboy boots? Add a pretend lasso and your little cowgirl will be ready to round 'em up!

Nothing completes an outfit like a pair of patterned tights or snazzy socks. Paint boldly striped tights, polka-dot tube socks, or even argyle knee-highs on your child—or let her paint them on herself.

Be sure to leave the soles of your child's feet paint free to avoid slipping and staining. Also, consider laying down newspaper or a large sheet of craft paper before you begin.

Note: This activity is not recommended on fabric, carpet, or delicate surfaces, as the paint might cause stains. Please take precautions to protect your flooring.

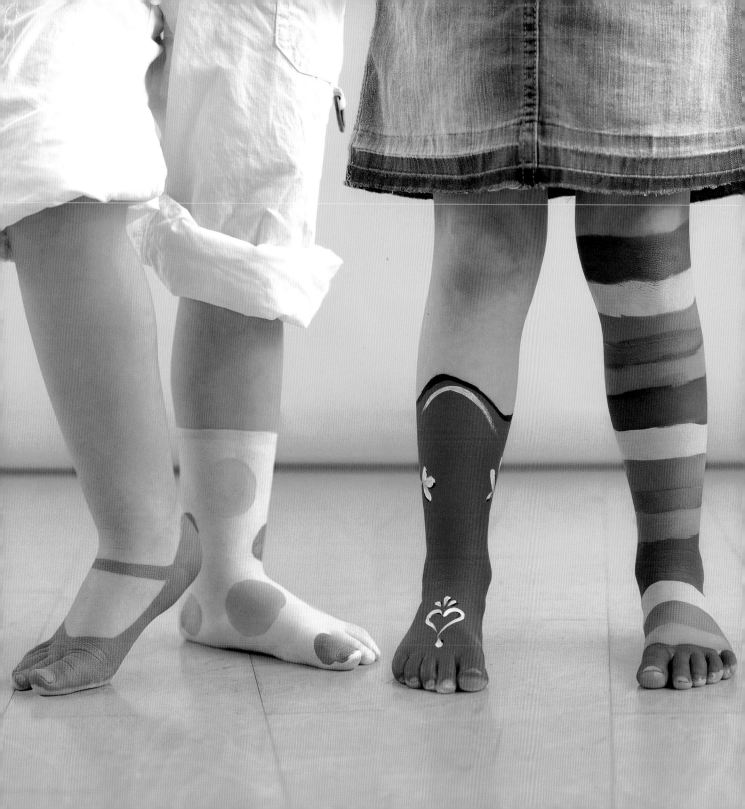

see the bubbles

To the tune of
"Mary Had a Little Lamb"

See the bubbles way up high,
Way up high, in the sky.
See the bubbles way up high,
Watch them floating by!

wonderbubbles

Kids always have big, big fun with amazing wonderbubbles: enormous bubbles made with a cone-shaped bubble blower.

Construct a cone by rolling heavy paper or a thin plastic sheet into a cone with a 3-inch (7.5-cm) opening at one end and secure it with strong tape. Dip the cone in the bubble solution, tap off the excess, blow steadily, and release an incredible wonderbubble with a quick, gentle flick of the wrist.

Children under four or so may need you to make the wonderbubbles for them, but older kids will most likely want to try their hand at making their own.

materials

- heavy paper or thin plastic sheets
- strong tape, such as packing tape
- bubble solution

found around

Becoming fluent in "crayon" is an important step in preliteracy. Encourage drawing and coloring by keeping crayons and washable markers in easy-to-grab containers and having plenty of paper of all sizes on hand. Clear ample scribble space on the floor or on a table. Then go on a treasure hunt with your young artist around the house, gathering everyday items that can be repurposed for interactive art projects.

Drape yarn or string on a large piece of paper and invite your child to color between the free-form lines and shapes. Talk about the tones and textures of different fabrics, and try to recreate them with crayons. Let coloring book pages tell a new story, cut up for a collage. Trace around the edges of cups or bowls to make patterns or use cookie cutters to make stencils. The artistic possibilities are endless!

sidewalk story

Ask your child to choose a favorite story, a fond memory, or an important event—such as a family vacation—to illustrate. Start off with a comic book–style template: he can use one sidewalk square per page or draw squares or rectangles in any size. Help your narrator present his tale in a logical order. Talk about the different parts of the story, who the characters are, what happens, and where things take place. This entertaining, graphic way to share a real-life anecdote encourages creative expression and builds literacy and memory skills.

we went on vacation

to the tune of "On Top of Spaghetti"

We went on vacation,
It was so much fun.
We rode on an airplane,
We played in the sun.
The beach was so sandy,
The water so blue.
We even went snorkeling,
There was so much to do!

throw a party

Tips

Party games promote physical skills such as hand-eye coordination, and social skills like being a good sport.

•

Involve your child in prep. She'll learn planning skills and contribute to the event.

•

Celebrating important milestones with loved ones lets your child know how special she is to you.

Parties are packed with chances for your child to enhance her developmental skills. Family and friends coming together to celebrate milestones, like birthdays, strengthens her identity. Gatherings also allow her to see herself in relation to others, practice social skills such as taking turns, and interact with both new and familiar faces. For young hostesses and hosts, sharing their parents with guests is great preparation for their growing independence.

shake, rattle & roll party

Get in the groove and help your child host a shake, rattle, and roll party where he and his friends are rock stars.

Make invitations by recording your child's favorite songs on CDs and writing the party information on each one. Or make CD-shaped invitations out of paper. On party day, have your child help set the scene with metallic streamers, add sparkle to star-shaped cupcakes or cookies, and put party favors (including cool shades) into decorated cups. Put out rockin' props, such as toy guitars and microphones.

For the main event, set up a stage inside or out. Have your child be the disc jockey and invite guests to sing along to the stereo or a karaoke machine. Kids can take turns putting on shows, or rock together in a giant jam session. Play rock 'n' roll oldies for background sound and freestyle dancing fun. Cheer and watch the little stars shine.

Jack

Rock Star

Rock Party

shake,
rattle,
and roll
party!!

for .... Aya's Birthday
date .... May 1st
from .... 2:00 PM to 4:00 PM

place .... The House of Rock & Roll
.... 5678 Jaybird Street
rsvp 555-4321

Aya's party playlist

Dancing on Sunshine
Video Rocked the Radio Star
99 Love Balloons
Loco Locomotion
Kung Pao Fighting
At the Bike Wash
Spunkytown

i am a rock star

To the tune of "B-I-N-G-O"

I am a rock star, yes I am.
See me sing and play.

Sing, sing, sing, and play,
Sing, sing, sing, and play,
Sing, sing, sing, and play,

'Cause that's what
rock stars do all day!

bubble party

Every budding bubble enthusiast loves a bubble party! So send out bubble-shaped invitations in fun envelopes (try paper CD sleeves), fill the party room with oodles of bubbles, and prepare some edibubble cupcakes with white and blue icing.

Blow, chase, and pop bubbles with all the party-goers. Stage a Bubblolympics with games such as dodge-a-bubble (page 64), bubble and spoon (page 70), and high jump, (page 81) as main events.

Give out small bottles of bubble solution, bubble-blowing wands, and bubble-shaped candies as party favors.

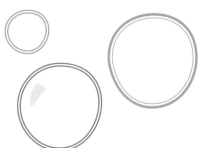

tiny bubbles

To the tune of
"Where Is Thumbkin?"

Tiny bubbles, tiny bubbles,
Yours and mine, yours and mine.
Make us all feel happy,
Make us all feel happy,
Make us feel fine,
Make us feel fine!

up, up, and away!
a superhero party

Help your masked wonder flex his superpowers and
throw an out-of-this-world party for his friends.

To make invitations, write the party details on speech bubbles
cut out of white paper and glued to brightly colored card stock.
Help your child create a poster-board cityscape of tall buildings,
and set up an obstacle course for the kids to leap around.

Offer the guests capes made out of colored pillowcases or
pieces of plastic tablecloth. Attach them with clothespins
or safety pins and stand back as the superheroes take off.
After they've saved the world several times over, the masked
marvels can refuel on crispy-rice treats cut into jagged bursts
and decorated with action words like "Pow!" and "Zap!"

twist and shout!
a dance party

Once your child has a few dance moves under his belt, help him host an old-fashioned sock hop. Make record-shaped invitations out of paper or vintage 45s with party details on the labels. Decorate the dance floor with black and white checks or other nostalgic patterns. Help your child make paper "records" to hang on the walls. Set up a drive-through on a table or counter and serve burgers, root-beer floats, and other malt-shop treats.

Help the boys roll up their pants and slick back their hair. Girls might like high, scarf-tied ponytails or wide headbands. Once everyone is ready, turn up the music and hand jive!

chalk party

Help your child throw a festive chalk party for her friends. She can decorate black construction paper or card stock to make "blackboard" invitations. Small boxes of chalk and miniature chalkboards (available at crafts stores) make great favors.

Welcome guests with a giant sign drawn on the sidewalk or front steps with arrows pointing to the fun. Trace the outline of each guest on a fence, garage door, or the side of a building to show the gathering crowd. Have the kids color themselves in to kick off the festivities.

Invite the guests to draw hopscotch or other game boards and play in small groups. Cover a table with paper and ask your guests to draw place settings, favorite foods, or whatever they'd like.

When your partygoers are wiped out from all the creative fun, fuel them up with "chalk-o-lat" milk and chalky-colored sherbet.

Skills Index

Index

Published by Fog City Press, a division of Weldon Owen Inc.
Produced by Weldon Owen Inc., 415 Jackson Street, San Francisco, CA 94111, USA,
in collaboration with Gymboree Play Programs, Inc., 500 Howard Street, San Francisco, CA 94105 USA.

Weldon Owen Inc.
Group Publisher, Bonnier Publishing Group **John Owen**
CEO and President **Terry Newell**
Senior VP, International Sales **Stuart Laurence**
VP, Sales & New Business Development **Amy Kaneko**

VP, Publisher **Roger Shaw**
Executive Editor **Elizabeth Dougherty**
Assistant Editor **Sarah Gurman**

Associate Creative Director **Kelly Booth**
Art Director **Lisa Milestone**
Senior Designer **Renée Myers**
Designer **Meghan Hildebrand**

Production Director **Chris Hemesath**
Production Manager **Michelle Duggan**
Color Manager **Teri Bell**

ISBN 978-1-74089-929-1
Library of Congress Control Number: 2009924563

Gymboree Play & Music
Chief Executive Officer **Matthew McCauley**
VP, Gymboree Play & Music **Jill Johnston**
Merchandise Manager **Dawn Sagorski**
Program Director & Contributing Editor **Gena Segno**

Additional Photography
Jennifer Pfeiffer pages 95 bottom right, 99, 104, 111, and front cover top inset. **Tosca Radigonda** pages 4 left, 8, 18–19, 27, 56–57, 64–65, 70–71, 74, 80, 93, 120–123, 128–129, 140–143, front cover bottom inset, and back cover bottom inset. **John Robbins** front cover.

Additional Text
Karen Penzes pages 18, 26–27, 56–57, 64, 70–71, 74–75, 80–81, 92–93, 120–121, 128–129, 140–141

Acknowledgments
Special thanks to Zero to Three for reviewing the content; Kristen Scott for face painting; Lisa Pfeiffer for chalk drawing and additional face painting on pages 95 bottom right, 99, 104, 111, and front cover top inset; Christine Coirault, Britt Staebler, and Malin Westman for illustrations; and Gaye Allen, design consultant.

Models

Jasper Baker, Hunter and Isabella Barbero, Mason Barnes, Gracie Bayne, Marina and Michael Belfiore, Isabella Bennett, Leo Berahovich, Carter Blair, Connor Bock, Kashan Bolton, Lydia Bradshaw, Sophia Bustamonte, Michaela Calvillo, Fiamma Carlone, Sophia Carrieri, James, Natalia, and Philip Churchley, Chloe Cervenka, Natalie Crafts, Camille Creighton, Anthony D'Aura, Molly Dinsmore, Emmarae Ensor, Camille Esterlechner, Emily and Olivia Fee, Ava Ford, Sophie Freitas, Eyal Garshon, Kate Griffin, Carson Hays, Zachary Hayward, Kristopher Holbert, Aya and Nami Kaneko, Grant Keffeler, Zachary Kirchstetter, Elijah Lagleva, Samantha Lee, Riley Low, Alma Margado, Kenyon and Ryon McMichael, Dashiell and Marisol Meier, Madison Metcho, Shailen Patel, Joseph Pinon, Caitlin Respicio, Logan Scribner, Giordana Simurdiak, Aurora Smith, Jaden Sonke, Charles Stanford, Emmett and Violet Stephens, Anna and Georgia Thomsen, Piper Todd, Elliot, Nora, and Oliver Vaughan, Devon Violante, Alexandra and Samantha Webber, Dayton and Valencia White, Zoe Wong-VanHaren, and Samantha Woollen.